HAVE A positive IMPACT...

...ON Others

by John Wood

KidHaven PUBLISHING

Published in 2025 by
KidHaven Publishing, an Imprint of
Greenhaven Publishing, LLC
2544 Clinton St., Buffalo, NY 14224

Written by: John Wood
Edited by: Rebecca Phillips-Bartlett
Designed by: Amelia Harris

Cataloging-in-Publication Data

Names: Wood, John, 1990-.
Title: On others / John Wood.
Description: Buffalo, New York : KidHaven Publishing, 2025. | Series: Have a positive impact… | Includes glossary and index.
Identifiers: ISBN 9781534547469 (pbk.) | ISBN 9781534547476 (library bound) | ISBN 9781534547483 (ebook)
Subjects: LCSH: Interpersonal relations--Juvenile literature. | Interpersonal communication in children--Juvenile literature. | Interpersonal relations in children--Juvenile literature. | Social interaction in children--Juvenile literature.
Classification: LCC HM1106.W66 2025 | DDC 302--dc23

Manufactured in the United States of America

CPSIA compliance information: Batch #CSKH25
For further information contact Greenhaven Publishing LLC at 1-844-317-7404.

Please visit our website, www.greenhavenpublishing.com.
For a free color catalog of all our high-quality books, call toll free 1-844-317-7404 or fax 1-844-317-7405.

Find us on

Contents

Words that look like this are explained in the glossary on page 31.

Who Are You Connected To?

Think of all the people you know. How many teachers do you know at school, and how many other students do you see every day? Do you have a big family, with aunts, uncles, brothers, and sisters? Or is it a small family? Think about all the people you see on the street, too.

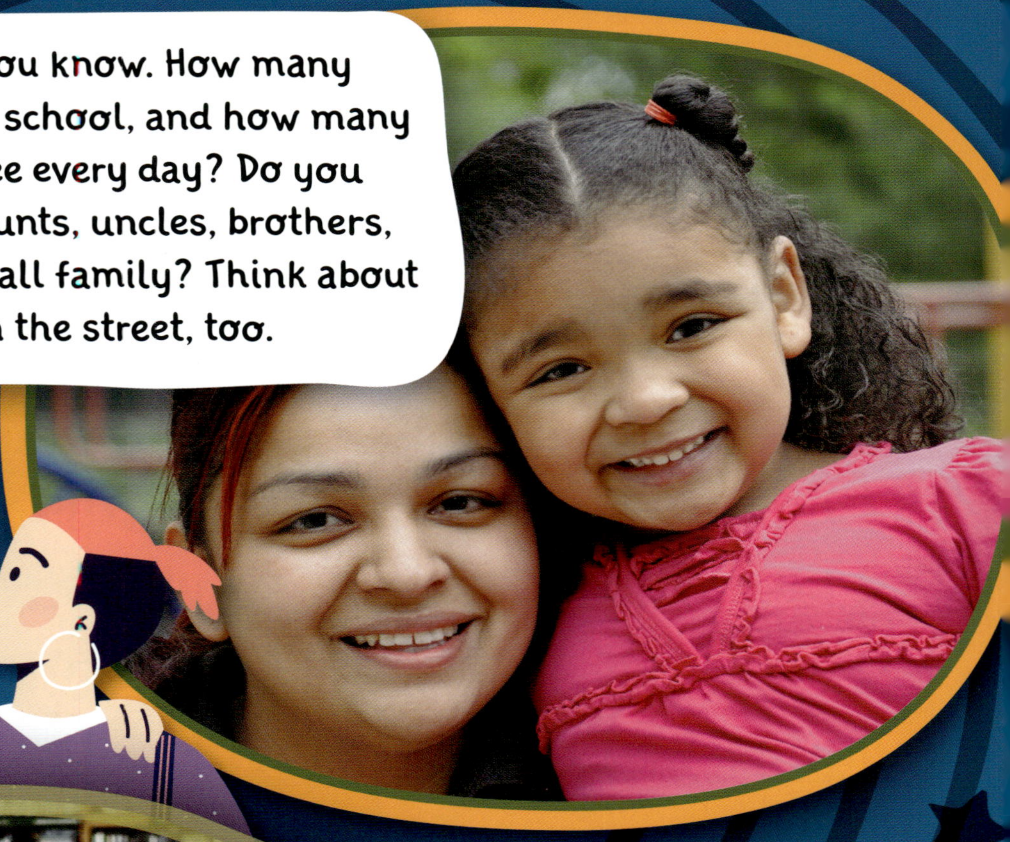

You might be surprised how many people you know when you count them up. You are connected to all these people, in one way or another. Some of them may be more important to you than others, but everyone you are connected to matters.

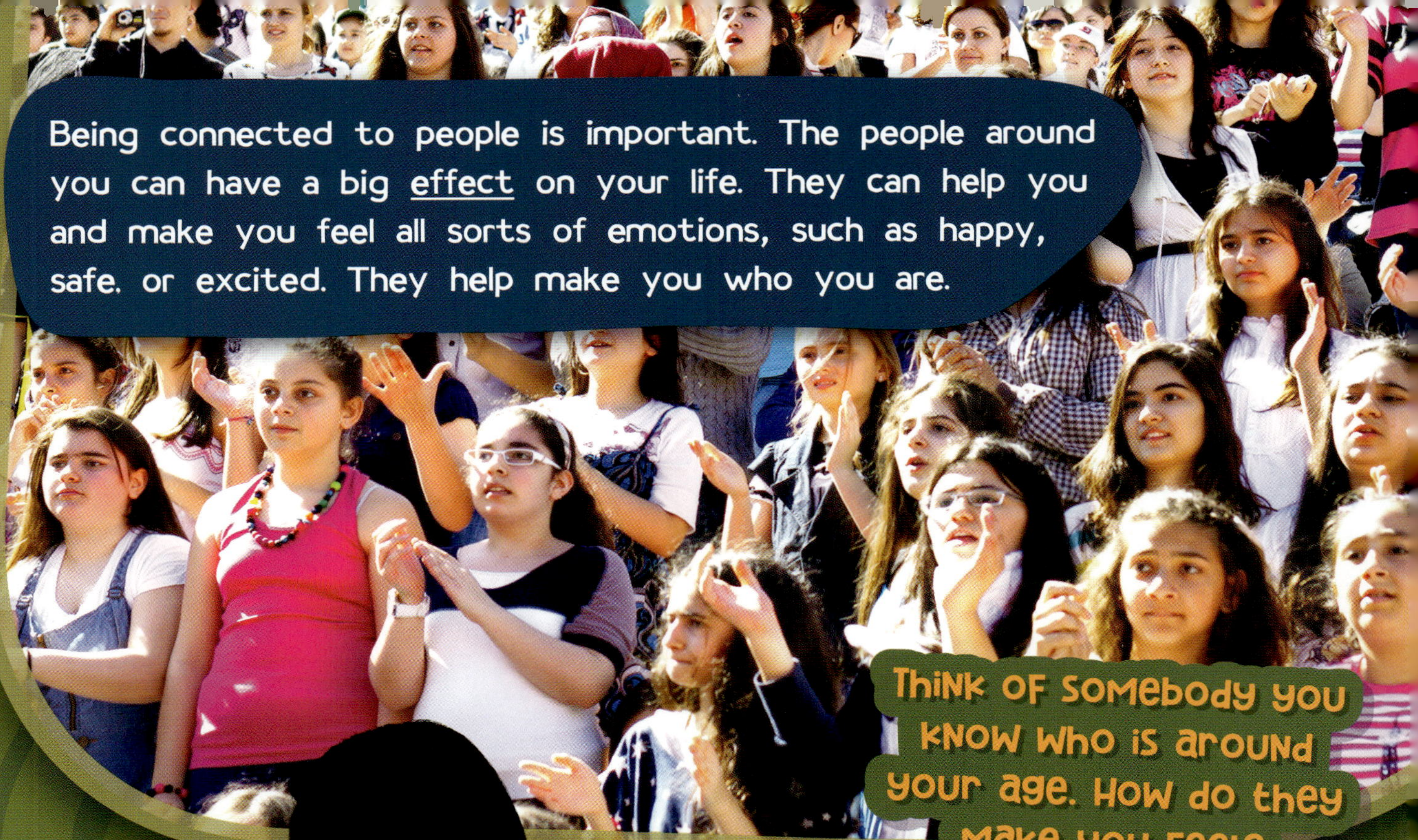

Being connected to people is important. The people around you can have a big effect on your life. They can help you and make you feel all sorts of emotions, such as happy, safe, or excited. They help make you who you are.

Think of somebody you know who is around your age. How do they make you feel?

Around the World

We are also connected with lots of people we've never met and might never know. These might be people online.

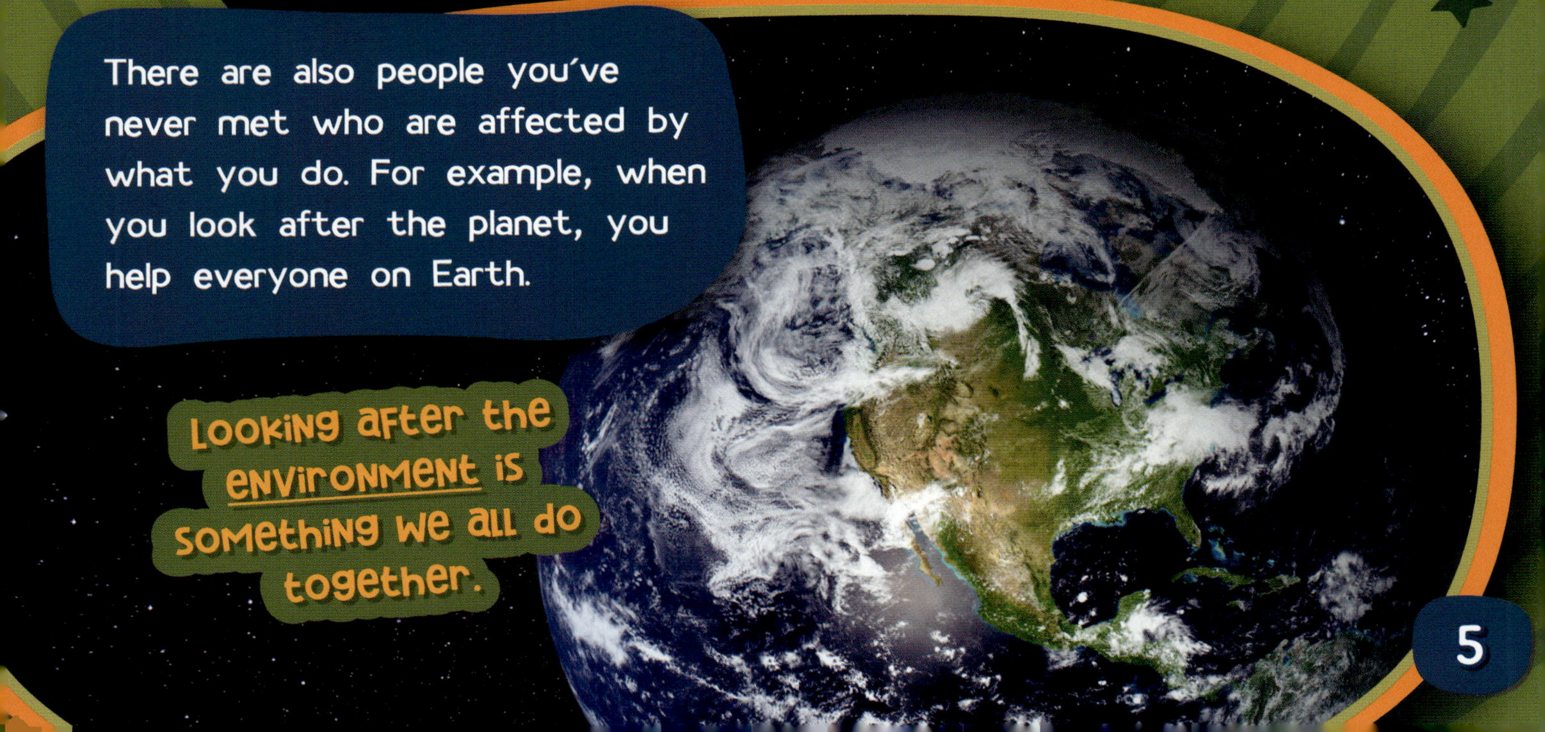

There are also people you've never met who are affected by what you do. For example, when you look after the planet, you help everyone on Earth.

Looking after the environment is something we all do together.

Feelings

Just as people are important to you, you are important to them. You have a big impact on the lives of everyone around you. The things you say and do can cause strong feelings in those you are connected to.

Everybody matters, and everybody makes a difference.

Can you think about a time when your words or actions have had an effect on someone else? What feelings do you think the other person felt?

Good Feelings

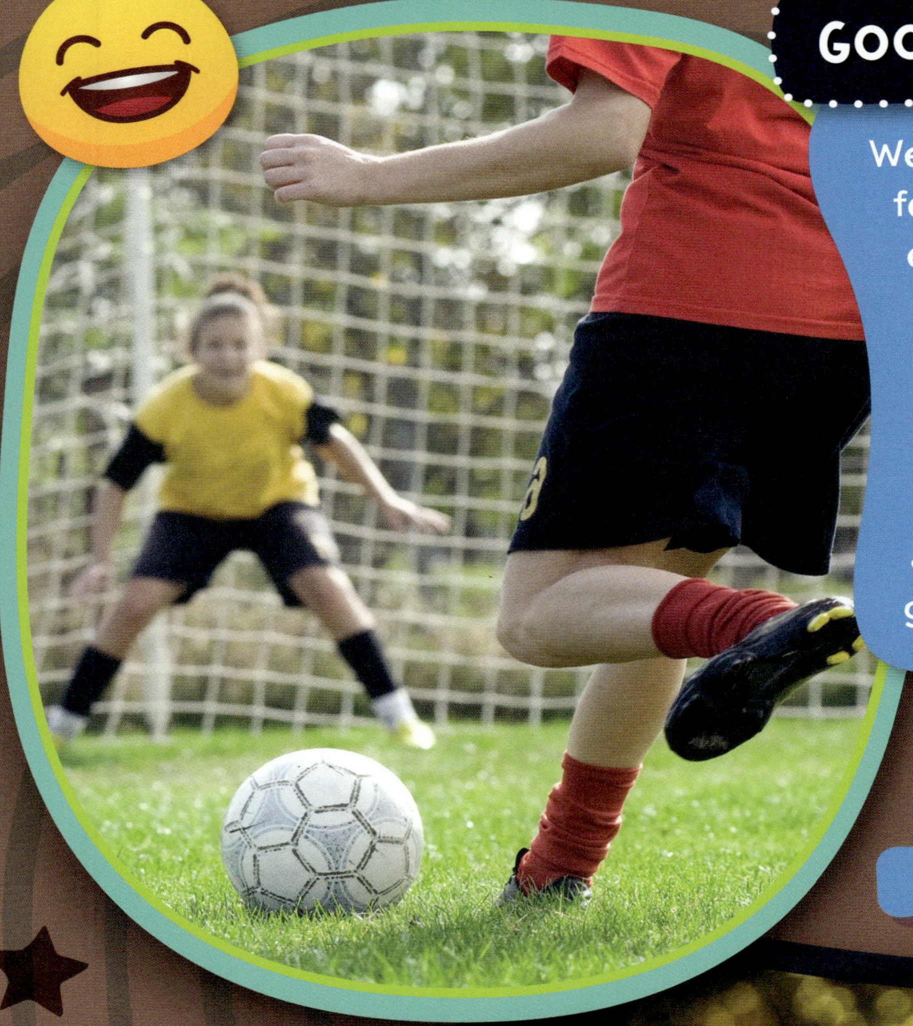

We all like to feel good feelings, such as happiness, excitement, love. and coziness. How do other people help to create those feelings in you? Perhaps it happens when someone cheers you on in a game or when someone gives you a compliment.

What are your favorite feelings?

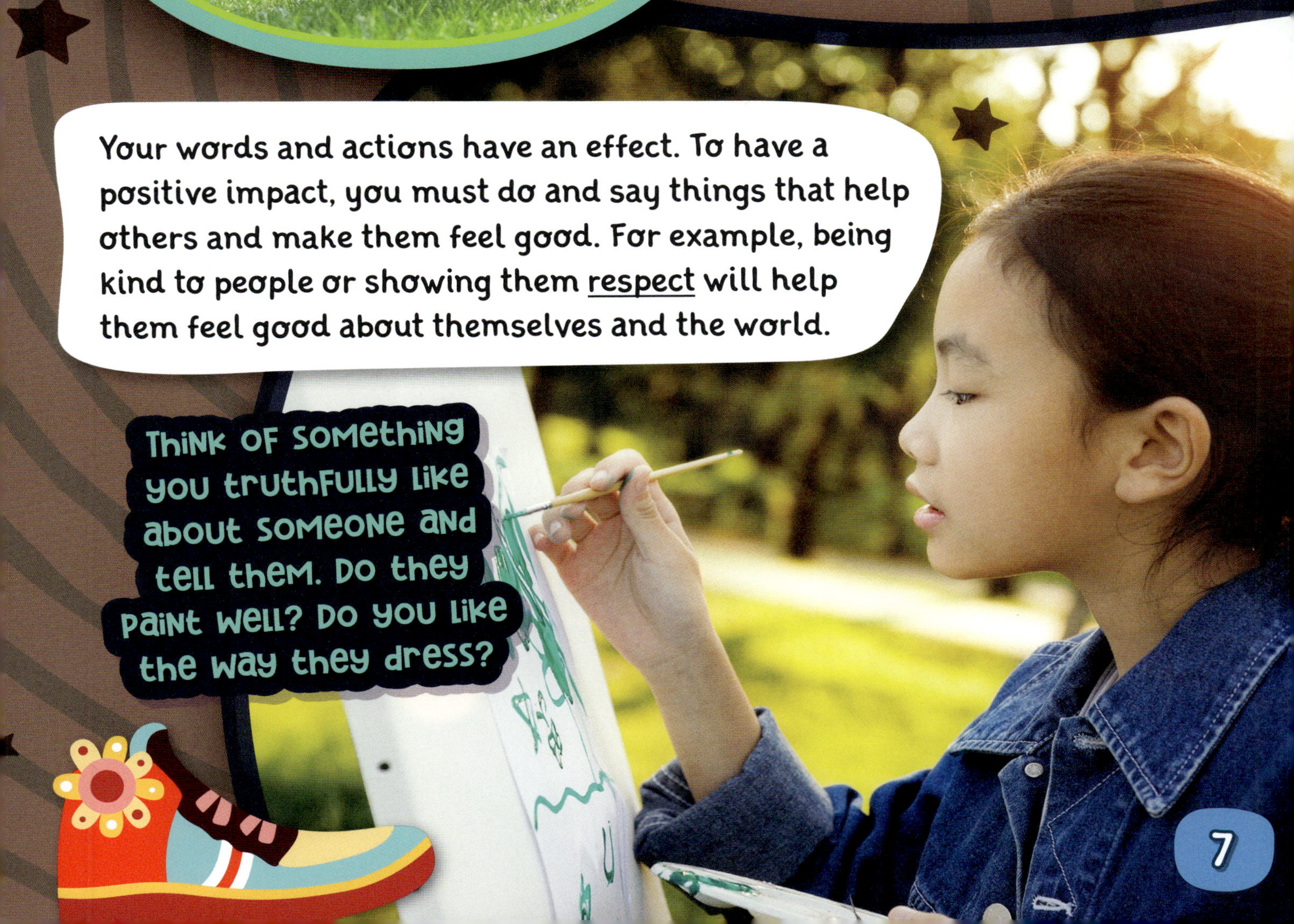

Your words and actions have an effect. To have a positive impact, you must do and say things that help others and make them feel good. For example, being kind to people or showing them respect will help them feel good about themselves and the world.

Think of something you truthfully like about someone and tell them. Do they paint well? Do you like the way they dress?

The Power of Words

Words are so important. The words we use can have a big impact on others. What kind of words could you use to make people feel good?

Good Manners

Having good manners means being polite and treating others with respect. While speaking to someone, it is good manners to say "please" and "thank you." You can also show kindness by not speaking too loudly and not interrupting people. Asking questions about someone can show them that you care.

Everyone communicates in their own way. People may have different ways of showing respect. Be kind and understanding by not judging someone for how they like to communicate.

Have a Positive Internet Impact

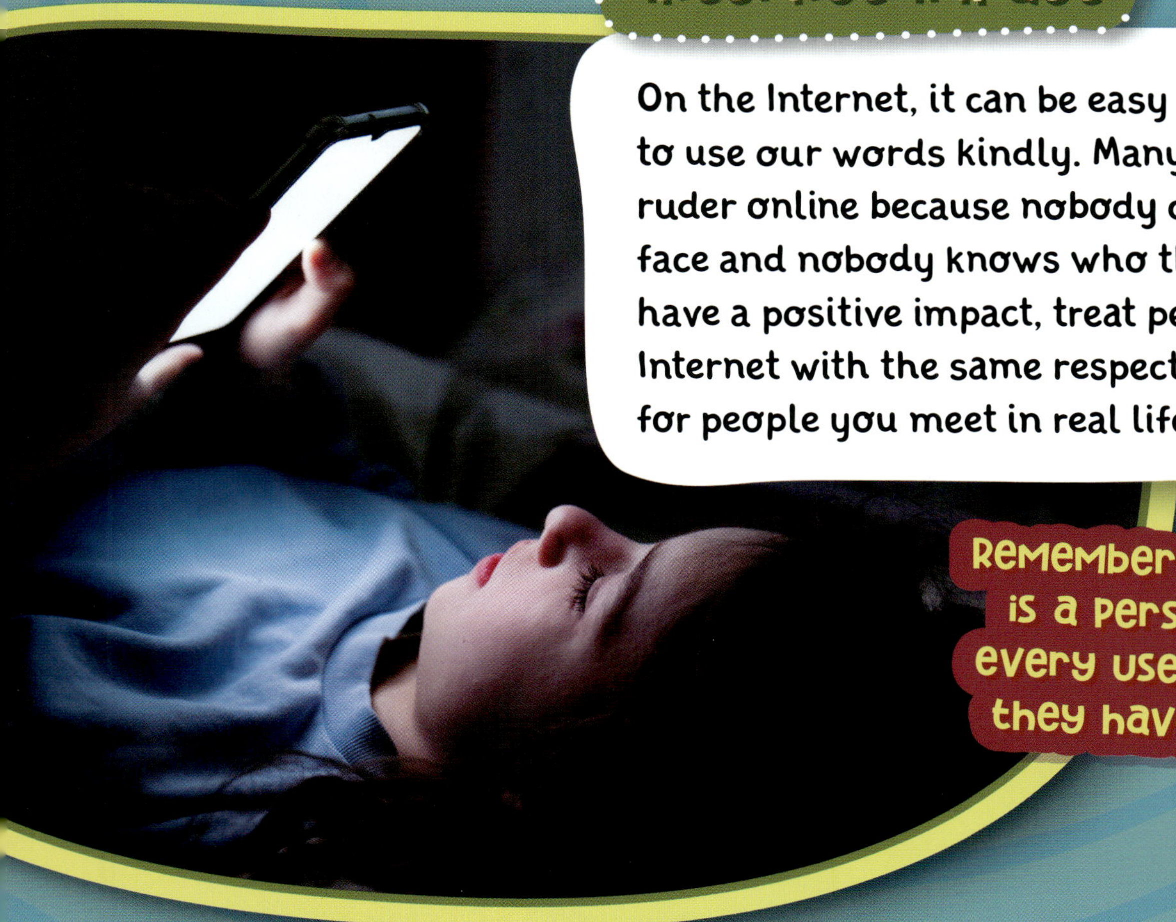

On the Internet, it can be easy to forget to use our words kindly. Many people are ruder online because nobody can see their face and nobody knows who they are. To have a positive impact, treat people on the Internet with the same respect you have for people you meet in real life.

Remember that there is a person behind every username, and they have feelings.

Listening

Sometimes, listening is better than talking. People often feel better when they have a chance to say their problems out loud, even if you don't know how to help them. It can feel good to be heard, which means you can help others just by listening.

Do you feel better when you tell someone your problems?

Active Listening

When listening to someone else's problems, it is important to listen well. When we listen carefully to really understand someone else, it is called active listening. You can have a positive impact on others by using active listening when they talk to you about their feelings and problems.

How to Listen

Listening is a skill. To get better at listening, try these things:

- Stop what you are doing and concentrate on the person and what they say
- Don't judge them and don't say what you think right away
- Look the person in the eye while they are speaking to you
- Really think about what the person is saying to understand their point of view
- Ask questions to help them talk about their feelings more
- You could repeat what they say in your own words to show you understand
- It is OK if there is silence — you don't have to rush to talk when they finish speaking

The Power of Actions

The words you choose and the ways you listen are both very important. However, sometimes these need to be followed by the right actions to have a positive impact. If you make a promise, you must keep that promise.

For example, if someone is feeling overwhelmed because they have so many chores and you tell them you can help them, you must follow that with helpful actions. If you listen to someone who is upset because everybody is too loud, you can take action by being quieter.

This brother and sister promised to help with the dishes.

Good Deeds

A good deed is an action that helps another person. Doing good deeds can be difficult, especially if it means giving something up or using your time on others. However, these actions can have a big positive impact.

Helping someone with their school project is an example of a good deed.

Touch

Some people like to be hugged or gently touched on the arm or back when they are upset. Hugs can be kind actions. However, make sure to ask before you give someone a hug or touch them in any way. Some people do not want to be touched, and it is important to understand and respect this.

What IS Empathy?

Empathy is the ability to imagine how other people feel. To use empathy, you have to really concentrate. Empathy is not about imagining how you might feel in someone else's situation. It is about thinking about how they actually feel in their situation. It can help to think about their personality and about things that have happened in their life.

EMPathy iSN't easy, aNd it takes Practice.

Empathy helps us understand each other. To help someone, you must understand them first. This is why empathy is so important in making the world a better place.

Empathy helps you understand how your words and actions will make another person feel. Knowing how someone else will feel will help you figure out the right thing to do.

Each person is unique. This is a good thing because it makes the world more interesting and fun. This is also the reason that empathy is so important to make sure everybody is treated well. Different people want different things and will react in their own way.

Empathy is your special power to help others.

Examples of Empathy

James and Isla

Isla is much quieter than usual today. After school, she usually likes playing video games with her friend James. However, today she says she can't. James imagines how Isla feels and wonders if she is upset. He remembers a time before when she was upset and spent the day alone. James thinks about it from Isla's point of view and thinks she needs time to be sad.

James wants to show that he cares, so he asks if she is OK. Isla doesn't say much, so he doesn't keep asking. Isla feels better the next day and thanks James for being kind and understanding how she felt.

Sam and Lila

Sam promised her sister, Lila, that she would play a game with her after school. Lila has been looking forward to it all week. However, Sam's friends are playing soccer in the park and ask if she wants to go. Sam wants to play soccer, but she thinks about how Lila would feel if she broke her promise.

She knows Lila would be too upset, so she keeps her promise and plays with her sister. Lila says Sam is the best big sister!

Putting It All INTO Practice

It's time to put everything you've learned into practice. Here are some ideas for small things you can do for those around you.

Help your parents with chores around the house. You could tidy up inside, wash the dishes after dinner, or help with the gardening.

Ask an adult how they are feeling and if they are enjoying their day. Use active listening when they give you their answer to show that you care about what they say.

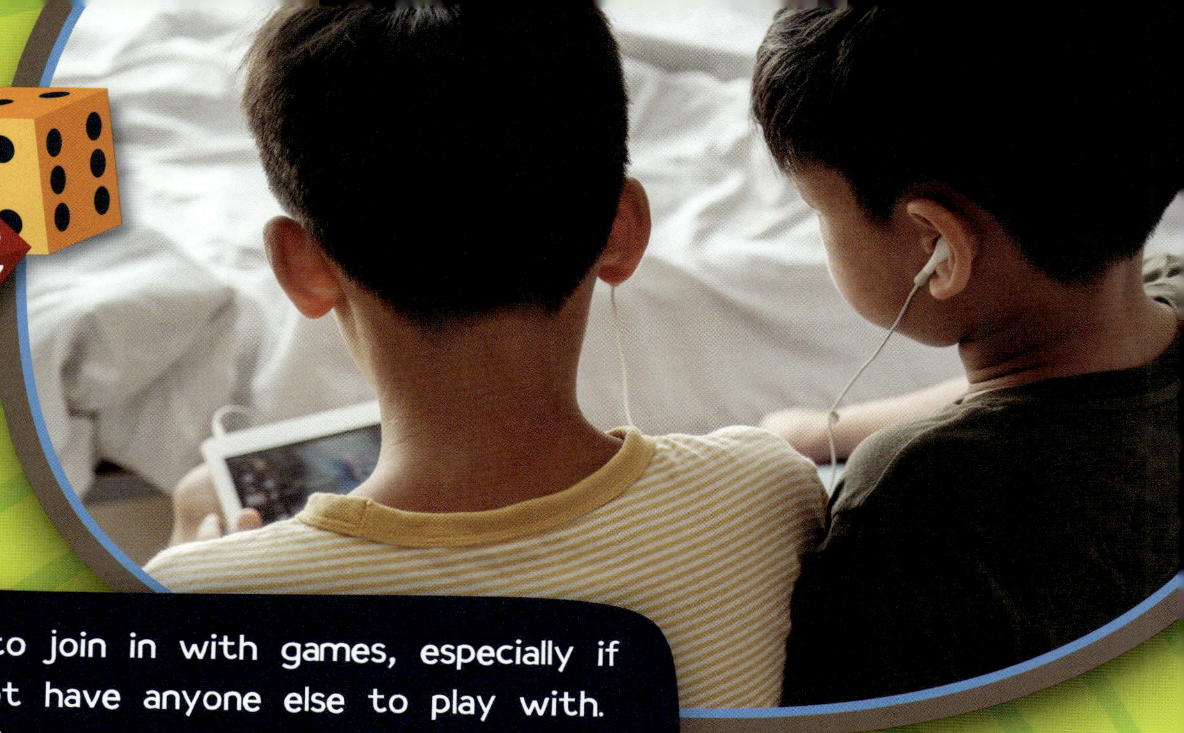

Invite others to join in with games, especially if they might not have anyone else to play with. You can also share your things with others, such as video game consoles or toys.

When you go through a door, it can be polite to hold it open for the person behind you.

If you are in line for lunch, let someone go before you. You could let your friends, brothers, or sisters have a turn on a shared computer or phone first.

Challenge Yourself

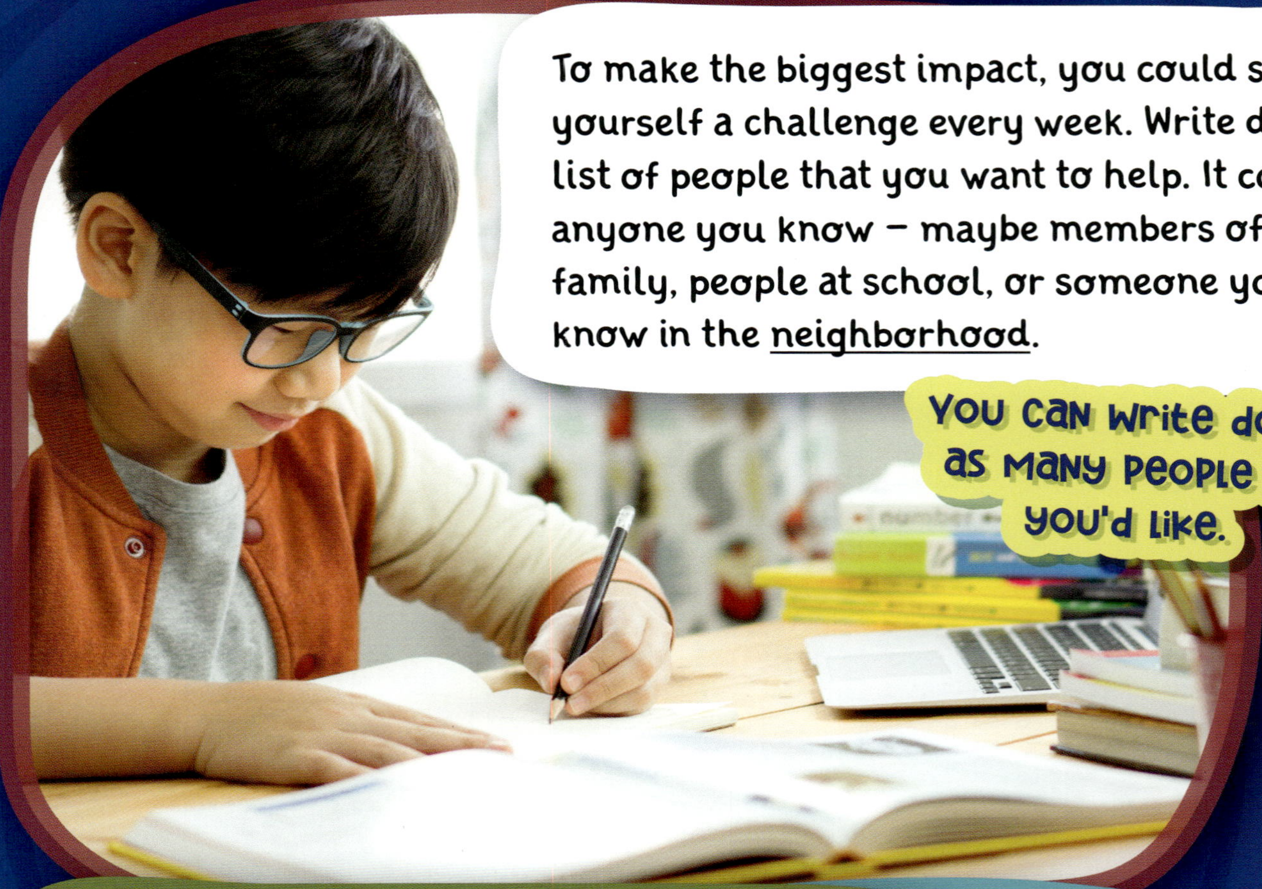

To make the biggest impact, you could set yourself a challenge every week. Write down a list of people that you want to help. It could be anyone you know – maybe members of your family, people at school, or someone you know in the neighborhood.

YOU CAN WRITE DOWN AS MANY PEOPLE AS YOU'D LIKE.

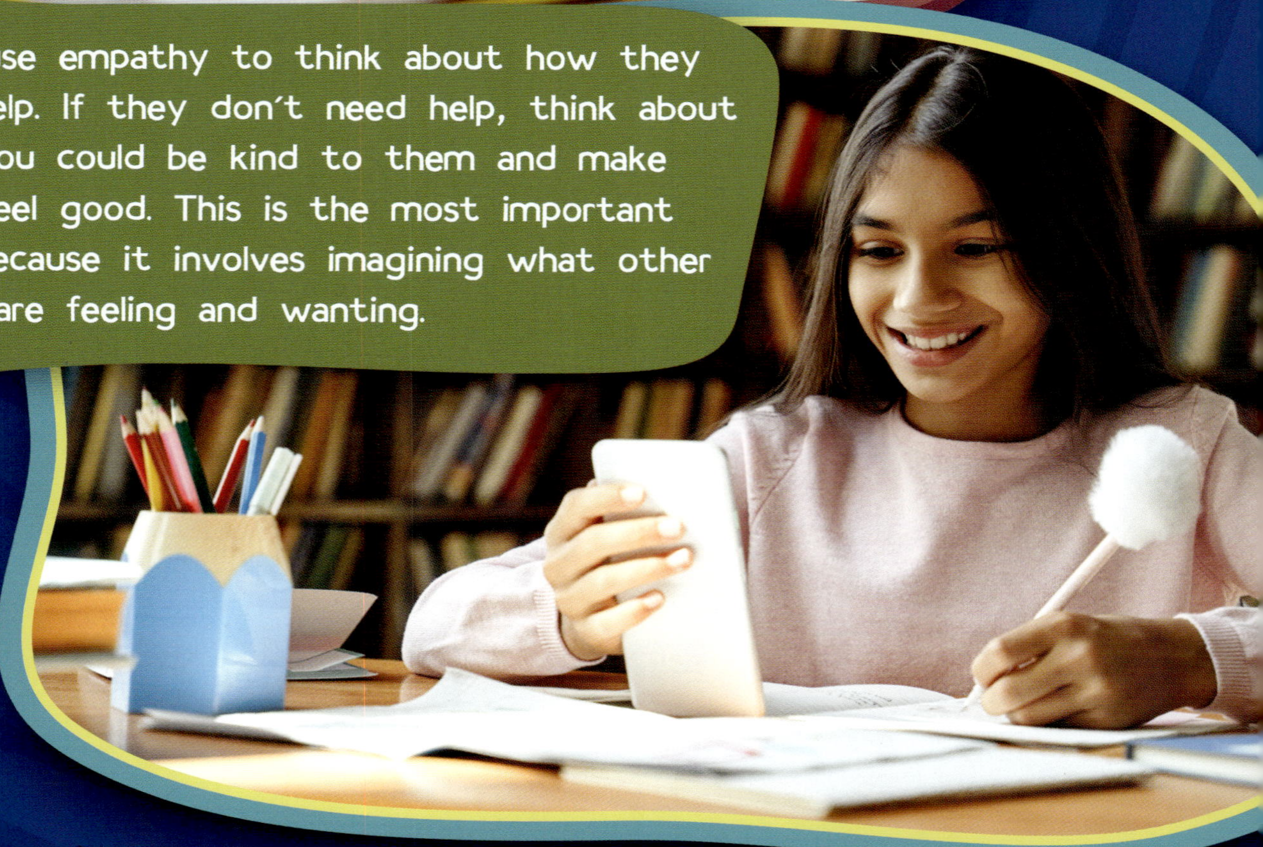

Next, use empathy to think about how they need help. If they don't need help, think about ways you could be kind to them and make them feel good. This is the most important part, because it involves imagining what other people are feeling and wanting.

You could even add people you do not know to your list. For example, you could try to help a stranger by donating food to a food bank.

Level Up

Now that you have your list and some ideas, challenge yourself to help at least one person a week. Think that is too easy? Set yourself an even bigger challenge and try to help a person on your list every single day!

Role Models

A role model is a person who sets a good example. Others usually look at role models to know how to behave. It is hard to know what to do all the time when you are young and still learning. Role models help you learn and grow up to be the best person you can be.

A role model might be a parent, a teacher, or even someone famous. Good role models have often tried very hard and overcome many difficulties. They are usually kind, and they help people.

Be Inspired

If you need more ideas on how to have a positive impact on others, look to your role model. How do they treat other people? How do they act in difficult times? Be inspired by your role model and try to learn from the positive things they do.

Future Role Model

Would you like to be someone's role model one day? Write down all the things you think make a good role model. What could you do to become that sort of person? If you are kind and respectful, and you help others, you could be a great role model in the future.

Giving to Others

What Is Charity?

Charity means giving help to groups of people who need it. A charity can also mean an organization that is set up to help people. Each charity has a purpose or a group of people it is trying to help. For example, some charities help rare animals, while others help fight certain diseases. There are charities to help people without homes, and there are charities for children who need help, too.

There are charities that help feed people who cannot afford food.

Charity is important because it is about helping people and the world, and not about making money.

Charities often help solve problems that aren't being solved by anyone else. They can do this because people give up their time, money, and possessions to help the charity.

Volunteering

Volunteering means giving up your time to do work for free. This is a great way to help others. For example, you could volunteer by picking up litter.

Some people volunteer in animal shelters, which look after animals that are hurt, sick, or need new owners.

Donations

When you give money or possessions away, it is called a donation. You can donate items you don't want to a charity. Food, such as cans of beans or soup, can be donated to food banks.

Jobs That Help People

Doctors and Nurses

Doctors and nurses help sick or injured people. They work in hospitals, doctors' offices, and other places where people need <u>medical</u> help. They have difficult but important jobs.

Counselors

Counselors help people who have difficulties with their emotions or <u>mental health</u>. They listen to people and use empathy to understand their problems. They can work in hospitals, schools, and community centers. Sometimes, they call people on the phone or speak over the Internet, too.

Charity Workers

Some people work for charities. There are lots of different jobs in charity, such as setting up events or speaking to people in public.

Aid Workers

Aid workers go to places that are affected by dangerous events, such as wars, natural disasters, or diseases. They help people who are in danger by taking food, water, medicine, and clothes to them.

Aid workers also help rebuild the area and train others.

Caregivers

Some people need help to live their day-to-day lives. This might be because of an illness, a disability, or because of their age. Caregivers can help people with everyday tasks, such as cooking, washing, and taking medicine.

Some caregivers work in care homes. Others visit a person's home to help.

Helping Feels Good

There are lots of reasons to help people. Helping people can feel good. Many people say that helping people puts them in a better mood. Scientists have even done studies to prove that this is true. Helping people is good for you!

It Goes Both Ways

Everyone needs help sometimes. There will be many days when you will need to ask for help, and there is nothing wrong with that. If you are the type of person who helps others, you will find that others want to help you.

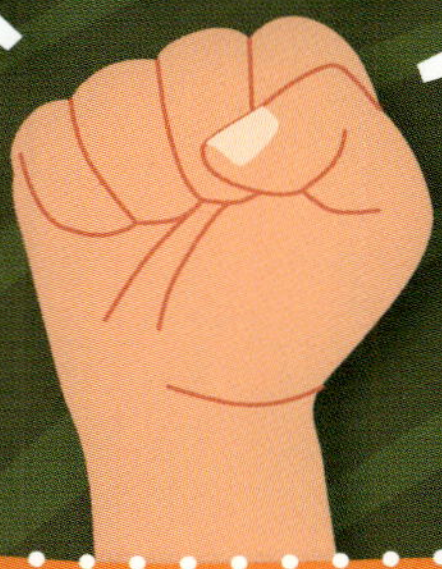

Power Up

Being kind and helpful will make everyone around you be the best they can be. Your positive impact will help your friends and family achieve greater and greater things, all thanks to you!

Out into the World

Making one person happy means that they are more likely to help someone else. This means that happiness can spread and spread, from one person to the next, all because of your good actions. You can think of it like dropping a stone into a pond and seeing the ripples spread to every corner.

A Positive World

Having a positive impact on others can change the world. It might not feel like it, but doing very small things here and there can make a huge difference.

Everyone is connected. There is no doubt that your words and actions do have an impact on others every day. The only question is: what kind of impact do you want to have on others?

Glossary

care homes places where people live together when they need extra help to keep them safe or complete everyday activities

compliment a nice thing said about someone

effect the result of an action or event

environment the natural world

food bank a place that gives out food for free to people who need it the most

inspired to be influenced by someone or something

judging having an opinion about something or someone

medical to do with medicine or treatment to cure injury and disease

mental health how well a person feels in their mind, and their ability to deal with stress

natural disasters events in nature that cause a lot of damage or harm, such as earthquakes

neighborhood a group of houses, buildings, people, and spaces that make up a small area in a town or city

organization a company, business, or charity formed for a particular purpose

possessions physical things that someone owns

public spaces that are open to people in the community

respect thinking good things about (or looking up to) someone or something

unique unlike anything or anyone else

Index

Image credits

All images are courtesy of Shutterstock.com, unless otherwise specified. With thanks to Getty Images, Thinkstock Photo and iStockphoto. Recurring images – imagewriter. Cover – ShineTerra, Lopolo, KHON SUPAN, Plateresca, nakaridore, Robert Kneschke. 2–3 – Studio Romantic. 4–5 – rSnapshotPhotos, Rawpixel.com, Rumka vodki, Faraways, metamorworks, 24K-Production, notbad. 6–7 – Brocreative, fizkes, SewCreamStudio, Fotokostic, anek.soowannaphoom, Studio Ladybug, BRO.vector. 8–9 – Prostock-studio, M_Agency, VLADGRIN, Olga Pink, Aleksandra Suzi, sulit.photos. 10–11 – shisu_ka, SeventyFour, lemono, fizkes. 12–13 – all_about_people, DGLimages, Ground Picture, WESTOCK PRODUCTIONS, VaLiza, Haali. 14–15 – myboys.me, OlhaTsiplyar, pizzastereo, fizkes, Roman Samborskyi, BRO.vector. 16–17 – Jacek Chabraszewski, StockImageFactory.com, Amanita Silvicora, etotishina. 18–19 – Vadim Zakharishchev, VH-studio, NotionPic, SewCreamStudio, Serhii Bobyk, Monkey Business Images, etotishina, masmas. 20–21 – myboys.me, Ground Picture, Rosamar, Steve Cukrov. 22–23 – Drazen Zigic, YAKOBCHUK VIACHESLAV, GoodStudio, Tartila, antoniodiaz, Eleonora_os, mantinov, Sudowoodo. 24–25 – addkm, Krakenimages.com, lemono, denayunebgt, Irina Strelnikova, hedgehog94, HASPhotos, Sameoldsmith, Quang Ho. 26–27 – Oleggg, Monkey Business Images, izo kat, FoxGrafy, littlenySTOCK, Vic Hinterlang. 28–29 – BearFotos, fizkes, OKADA_jp, HappyPictures, lemono, jordanxavr, ivector, sachch. 30–31 – TinnaPong, NicoElNino, Felink - Creative Studio.